A Book about a Boy WHO IS BLIND

T. J.'s Story

Text and photographs by Arlene Schulman

Ŀ LERNER PUBLICATIONS COMPANY / MINNEAPOLIS

Acknowledgments
The author wishes to thank James Lien; Dr. Laurence R. Gardner, Director
of Educational Services for the New York City Board of Education; Iris
Torres, Coordinator of the Vision Resource Center of the New York City
Board of Education; and Mark H. Leeds, Director of the New York City
Mayor's Office for People with Disabilities, for their assistance.

Website address: www.lernerbooks.com

LIBRARY OF CONGRESS CATALOGING-IN-PUBLICATION DATA

Schulman, Arlene.
    T.J.'s story : a book about a boy who is blind / text and photographs
by Arlene Schulman.
        p. cm.
    Includes bibliographical references.
    Summary: A nine-year-old boy who has been blind from birth
describes various aspects of his life, including his reading in Braille, his
use of a cane, and the games he plays with his friends.
    ISBN 0-8225-2586-0 (alk. Paper)
    1. Olsen, T. J. (Thomas Joseph) —Juvenile literature. 2. Children,
Blind-United States—Biography—Juvenile literature. 3. Blindness—
Juvenile literature. [1. Blind. 2. Physically handicapped.] I. Title.
HV1596.3.S38 1998
362.4'1'09—dc21
    [B]   97-25129
Manufactured in the United States of America
1 2 3 4 5 6 – JR – 03 02 01 00 99 98

CONTENTS

MY NAME IS T.J. Olsen. You can see me, but I can't see you. That's because I'm blind.

People who are blind can see very little or nothing at all. Some people are born blind. Others lose their sight when they get older because of illnesses such as glaucoma and diabetes. I was born with a disease called retinoblastoma. It's a kind of cancer. It affects babies when they're born.

When I was 11 months old, doctors had to do surgery to get rid of the cancer. They removed my eyes. Instead of real eyes, I have plastic ones. Most people don't know that I'm blind until they see me with my cane. It's white and red and it looks like a walking stick.

Your eyes work like a camera. There is a lens at the front of each eye. The lens focuses on what you're seeing. The colored part of the eye, called the iris, opens and closes to let in the right amount of light. At the back of the eye is the retina. It's like the film in a camera. It records a picture of what you see.

Many people wear eyeglasses because their eyes don't work perfectly. They may not be able to see things far away or close up very well. Normal eyeglasses aren't enough for people who are visually impaired or blind. Their eyesight cannot be corrected with regular eyeglasses.

People who are visually impaired or blind may be able to see some things, like shapes or light and dark objects or very large things. In the United States, more than a million people are blind. More than nine million are visually impaired. Blindness is more serious than visual impairment.

You might think you can close your eyes and pretend you're blind. But you've already seen things around you, so you can picture them in your mind. I can't. I don't know what the color red is or what a tree looks like. I can't tell how tall or short someone is or if something is beautiful or ugly. I've never seen my house or my brothers or my mom and dad. I don't even know what I look like. But I can feel the shape of things, like a basketball or a cupcake or a desk. I can feel if something is soft or hard, fuzzy or smooth. I can listen to the sounds of voices and music.

It doesn't really matter that I can't see. This is the way a lot of other people are, and this is the way I am. I like being the way I am. There is an old saying, "A blind man who sees is better than a seeing man who is blind."

I'M THE OLDEST child in my family. I'm nine years old. I'm named after my father. He's Thomas Francis, and I'm Thomas Joseph. I'm called T.J., so people can tell us apart. I have two younger brothers. Andrew is six and Mark is four. Mark is nice, but you know how little kids are. Sometimes he doesn't like to get dressed. Andrew is pretty independent. He likes to play basketball and play in the park. Andrew and I leave our radios tuned to stations that have kids' programs.

7

We live on Staten Island. It's one of the five boroughs of New York City. (Boroughs are different sections of the city—Manhattan is the most famous.) Staten Island is separated from Manhattan by five miles of water. You can only get to Staten Island by bridge or ferry. You can see the Statue of Liberty from some parts of Staten Island.

My father sells advertising for billboards. He has his own company, and he works at home. My mother works for a company that lends money to people who buy big buildings. She gets up at 5:30 in the morning to get us ready for school. She cooks breakfast for us. It's usually cereal or eggs, and once in a while she makes pancakes. My mom and dad both make lunch for us. My dad bakes pretty good brownies.

Mark, Andrew, and I all go to different schools. My parents go to all of our teachers' meetings and PTA meetings. Sometimes Mom makes cupcakes for everyone in my class.

When I get dressed for school, my mother picks out my clothes for me. I can tell the difference between corduroy and jeans and wool, but I don't know what color anything is. When I get a little older, my clothes will be sorted with pins with raised plastic dots on them so I will know which clothes go together. One dot might mean that the shirt is blue, and two could mean red.

I'M IN FOURTH GRADE at the Michael J. Petrides Public School in Staten Island. Our teacher is Mrs. McDonald. I really like Mrs. McDonald and the kids in my class. Everyone in my class helps me out. They tell me how to get to my desk. If I lose a book, they find it for me.

We do a lot of fun stuff in Mrs. McDonald's class. We write in our journals, and we solve the math problem of the day. We're learning to spell words like Staten Island. And we're reading about the Cherokee Indians.

I read in Braille. The Braille alphabet is made up of raised dots arranged in different patterns. They stick up on the paper so I can feel them with my fingers. The Braille alphabet was invented by a French man named Louis Braille in the 1820s. You read Braille by running your hands along the pages. Sometimes just one dot or one letter can mean a whole word. Like, a "c" equals "can" and "p" means "people." When I read from one of my textbooks in Braille for the first time, everyone in class clapped.

On the first day of school, I printed all my classmates' names in Braille on my Perkins Braille writer. It's like a portable typewriter, except that it has Braille keys. When everyone else takes notes with a pen and paper, I use a Braille 'n' Speak. It's like a little computer. It's quieter than the Perkins Braille writer. I type in some commands and it plays my notes back in a voice. When I hook it up to a printer, it can print in Braille or in the regular alphabet. I taught myself to use the Braille 'n' Speak.

13

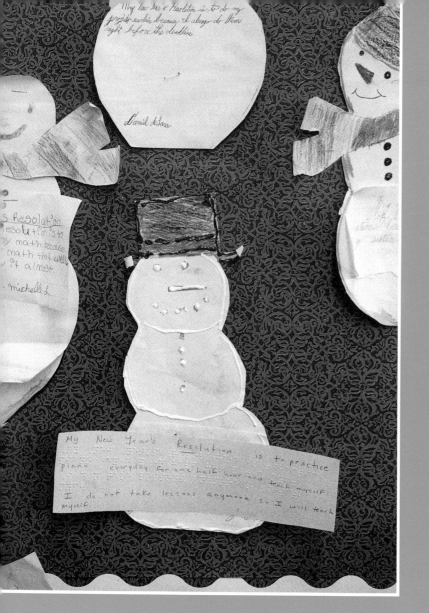

I also have a talking calculator. Pretty soon I'll be getting a computer that has software with talking commands. With computers, I can't use a mouse or programs that use graphics. I will use voice commands to tell the computer what to do.

I can label things in Braille with a Braille labeler. When I'm a little older, I'll learn how to fold money so that I can tell the difference between a five-dollar bill and a ten-dollar bill. Right now I can't tell if someone at a store gives me the right change or not, but most people are honest.

An educational assistant named Ann Eadicicco goes with me to every class. I call her Miss E. She makes sure that I have the class work in Braille and that I'm able to follow along with the other kids. Fran Bambara is my Braille teacher. She gets the homework assignments from Mrs. McDonald at the beginning of the week and translates them into Braille. Then, when I hand in my homework, she translates it back for Mrs. McDonald. I can write my name like everyone else. But for me and most people who are blind, the regular alphabet is just as foreign as Braille would be to a person who can see.

Most of the time, I leave my classes five to ten minutes early with Miss E so I don't get trampled. You know how the hallways are in school—crowded. Other times, I walk with Linda Lee, who's in my class. We talk about what books we've read. I like to read. One of my favorite books is *Stealing Home*. It's about a boy and his grandfather and an aunt who drives them crazy. I read *Ramona and Her Mother* by Beverly Cleary. I'm a big fan of hers. And I like the "Goosebumps" books.

My books are on cassette or they're in Braille. I get books in Braille from the Andrew Heiskell Library for the Blind and Visually Impaired. It's part of the New York Public Library in Manhattan. I order five books at a time and they send them to me in the mail. They come in a big box. The cassettes are from the Library of Congress. To listen to them, I have to use a special four-track tape recorder. There are magazines and newspapers in Braille, like *Discover*, The *Washington Post Book World,* and computer magazines. You can even get *Playboy* in Braille, but my mother won't let me read that!

My favorite subject is science. We do a lot of experiments. Michael Hagar, who sits next to me, helps me. My worst subject is math. Math is so hard. A lot of the problems are very long.

In art class, I have a drawing board and special glossy paper. I trace designs with a special tool sort of like a pizza wheel. It makes marks in the paper that I can feel. I can cut and paste by myself. Another class I like is Spanish. I'm in my first year.

Gym class is fun. We go outside and practice dribbling. I have a ball with bells inside so I can keep track of it. The class is divided into one section for girls and one for boys. Mr. Duffy calls us "gentlemen" and we start by doing sit-ups and push-ups. Tom Downing is a really good basketball player. He likes to play basketball with me.

MY BEST FRIEND is Heather Nelson. We've known each other since kindergarten. She's fun to play with, and we go trick-or-treating together on Halloween. I also like to go to the park with my brother Andrew, and we like to play Scrabble, chess, and Battleship. We play Monopoly with Heather, my friend Douglas, and the two girls who live next door, Marisela and Carla. All these games have instructions and game pieces in Braille. There's even Monopoly money in Braille.

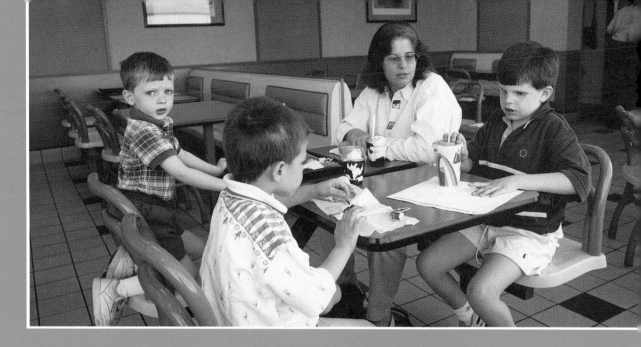

Other things I like to do are swimming, in-line skating, and listening to TV. I go swimming at the Staten Island YMCA. I skate in front of my house or at the park with one of my parents. At home, I listen to videos that have special descriptions of what's happening on the screen. When I eat at McDonald's, they have Braille menus. The lids of the cups have Braille on them, too, so I know what I'm drinking. I like shopping at Nordstrom because all their signs are in Braille. And in church, I can read along with a Braille mass book.

I also like music. My favorite is classical—Tchaikovsky and Beethoven. I have a collection of tapes of music by different composers. In my music class, we all sing while the teacher plays the piano.

For about three years, I've been taking piano lessons at The Manhattan Lighthouse for the Blind with Mr. Sanfilippo. He's blind, too. The notes of the musical scales are written in Braille on the sheet music. I like to play the piano and sing. I'm learning the song "My Bonnie Lies over the Ocean."

One of my favorite places to go is the Liberty Science
Center in Jersey City, New Jersey. That's just over the bridge
from Staten Island. The center has exhibits on three floors.
It's so cool—I can touch everything. I can feel how the
human heart and brain work by touching models of them.
I can feel how gears move and I can hold snakes and bugs.
Everyone in my family loves to climb the fossilized rock wall
at the center.

A BLIND PERSON relies on touch. When I walk outside of my house, I use a cane. It's called a California cane, because that's where it's made. I've been using it since I was four. I sweep the floor from side to side with the cane. I can get a sense of touch with it—I can feel the ground through the cane.

A man named John Stevenson taught me how to use my cane. He's a mobility instructor. He teaches me to count steps going up or down stairs and how to cross the street. There's nothing wrong with stumbling or bumping into things. Everyone does it, even people with perfect vision.

After I graduate from high school, I'll probably get a guide dog. Guide dogs are trained to help blind people. My dog will be a Labrador, a golden retriever, or a German shepherd. I can't get a dog yet, because I'm still learning and the dog would be bigger than I am.

A law called the Americans with Disabilities Act was passed in 1990. The law makes it easier for me and other people with disabilities to use public buildings and transportation. Cuts in street curbs make it easier for people in wheelchairs to cross the street. The cuts also let me know where the street corner is.

A big adventure for me is learning to ride the New York City subway. It's actually a big adventure for anybody. There are so many stations and people pushing and shoving. I'm too young to go by myself, so I go with John, my mobility instructor. On the subway platform, it's best to be in contact with the wall at all times. At most stations, the edge of the platform has plastic tiles that keep you away from the tracks below. People who use guide dogs use their feet to tell them where they are. John and I use a subway map with Braille markings and a talking compass.

There are all sorts of equipment to help people like me. There's a "mini reader" system that can read labels and price tags. A Noteller scans and reads money. You can get all kinds of talking things—a talking dictionary, fax machine, clocks, watches, scales, even a talking thermometer.

Every blind person is different. There's a disc jockey who is blind. There are blind runners. Blind people can wrestle, play golf, go rock climbing, canoeing, horseback riding, and whitewater rafting. Some blind people study karate and others ski. Blind people vote in elections. In New York, someone goes into the booth with you to push the levers.

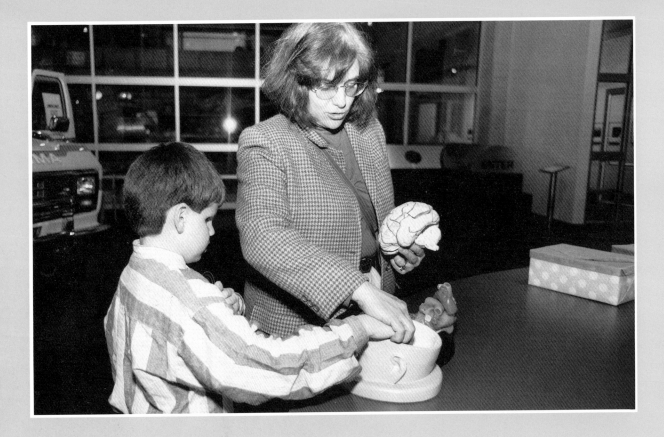

Helen Keller was a famous blind person. She was also deaf. She inspired a lot of people. She was a writer and she gave talks about the challenges of being blind and deaf. Blind people can play instruments, become attorneys, writers, politicians, librarians, psychologists, teachers, scientists, computer programmers—almost anything.

I plan to go to college. Thousands of kids who are blind or visually impaired go to college. My mom wants me to be a lawyer. Maybe I'll even be a judge. Justice is supposed to be blind! But I really don't know yet. I still have a long time to decide.

Information about **BLINDNESS**

When a person is blind, as T.J. is, he or she has very little or no vision. The problem cannot be corrected with regular eyeglasses. The legal definition of blindness is vision of 20/200 or less with glasses. What this means is that if someone with excellent vision could see an eye chart clearly from 200 feet (62 meters), a blind person could only see the chart clearly from 20 feet (6.2 meters).

Blindness can be caused by injury or by a disease of the eyes or brain. A baby may be blind at birth. People may lose their sight as they get older. Diseases such as glaucoma and diabetes can cause loss of vision.

People who are visually impaired can usually see something. They may be able to make out shapes or see things up close. Still, their vision is more limited than people who wear regular eyeglasses. People who can see are referred to as "sighted."

People who are blind or visually impaired may use a cane or a guide dog to help them. (Guide dogs are also called Seeing Eye Dogs.) They often use special computers, typewriters, calculators, thermometers, clocks, maps, and watches.

Sometimes children attend special schools for the blind, but many blind children go to school with sighted children. In 1975, a law was passed requiring that children with a disability receive a free education. Students like T.J. do the same class work, homework, and tests as other students in their classes. Class work, textbooks, and tests may be adapted into Braille or put on audio cassettes. In gym classes, basketballs, footballs, and soccer balls are made with bells inside so a blind student can hear when the ball is thrown. Books, magazines, and games are often available in Braille.

The Americans with Disabilities Act was passed in 1990. It protects people with disabilities from discrimination. Public places like stores, restaurants, movie theaters, hotels, and parks must be able to be used by people who are disabled. It is also illegal to discriminate against someone who has a Seeing Eye Dog. The dog is not considered a pet and is allowed to travel everywhere with its owner.

There is no cure for blindness. But technology is always improving. One day someone may invent an electronic eye that will give T.J. and others sight.

The photographs on pages 36-37 are of T.J. and his classmates.

GLOSSARY

blind—unable to see

blindness—partial or complete loss of sight that cannot be corrected with ordinary eyeglasses. Blindness is generally considered to be less than one-tenth of normal vision.

Braille (BRAYL)—a system of writing and printing that uses an alphabet made up of raised dots arranged in different patterns. Louis Braille was born in Paris in 1809 and developed a military code that was used by soldiers to communicate after dark. The code was then adapted for use by blind people. Braille himself was blind from the age of three.

cancer—a serious, sometimes deadly, growth of cells in the body. It is usually treated by surgery and chemicals.

diabetes (DYE-uh-bee-teez)—a disease in which there is too much sugar in the blood. Diabetes can lead to blindness.

disability—a limitation that interferes with a person's ability to function—for example, to see, walk, learn, talk, or hear

discrimination (dis-CRIM-ih-NAY-shun)—unfair treatment based on something such as disability or race

eye—an organ of sight

glaucoma (glaow-COH-muh)—a disease of the eye

guide dog—a dog trained to lead the blind; also called Seeing Eye Dog

iris (EYE-riss)—the round, colored part of the eye

lens (lenz)—the part of the eye that focuses light rays

mobility—the ability to move

retina (RET-uhn-uh)—the lining at the back of the eye that receives the images produced by the lens and sends them to the brain

retinoblastoma (RUH-tee-noh-blast-OH-muh)—a cancer of the eyes

visually impaired—a severe loss of vision

RESOURCES

American Blind Lawyers Association
Box 1590
Indianola, MS 38751
(601) 887-5398

American Council of the Blind
1155 15th Street NW, Suite 720
Washington, DC 20005
(202) 467-5081

American Foundation for the Blind
11 Penn Plaza, Suite 300
New York, NY 10001
(212) 502-7600

Helen Keller International
90 Washington Street, 15th Floor
New York, NY 10006
(212) 943-0890

The Lighthouse Inc.
111 E. 59th Street
New York, NY 10022
(800) 334-5497

The National Eye Institute
Office of Health Education and
    Communication
Building 31, Room 6A32
Center Drive MSC 2510
Bethesda, MD 20892-2510
(301) 496-5248

National Braille Association
3 Townline Circle
Rochester, NY 14623-2513
(716) 427-8260

Research to Prevent Blindness
645 Madison Avenue, 21st Floor
New York, NY 10022-1010
(800) 621-0026

U.S. Department of Justice
Civil Rights Division
Disability Rights Section
P. O. Box 66738
Washington, D.C. 20035-6738
(800) 514-0301   TDD (800) 514-0383

For Further READING

Alexander, Sally Hobarth. *Mom Can't See Me.* New York: Macmillan, 1990.

Brink, Ben. *David's Story: A Book about Surgery.* Minneapolis: Lerner Publications, 1996.

Goldstein, Margaret J. *Eyeglasses.* Minneapolis: Carolrhoda Books, 1997.

Landau, Elaine. *Blindness.* New York: Twenty-First Century Books, 1994.

Parker, Steve. *Living with Blindness.* New York: Franklin Watts, 1989.

About the
AUTHOR
AND
PHOTOGRAPHER

Arlene Schulman is an award-winning journalist and photojournalist who lives in New York City. She is the author of *Carmine's Story: A Book about a Boy Living with AIDS* and *Muhammad Ali: Champion,* as well as a book for adults, *The Prizefighters: An Intimate Look at Champions and Contenders.* Her work has appeared in *The New York Times,* The New York *Daily News,* The *New York Post,* and other publications. Her photographs can be found in The New York Public Library, the Museum of the City of New York, The Westinghouse Corporation, and private collections.